KT-460-301

On the Trail of the American Indians

What kind of people lived in North America before the white men came?

6

Redskins

What do you think of when you hear the words 'Red Indians'? Tomahawks, tepees, smoke-signals? War-bonnets, bows and arrows, pipes of peace? That's the picture of native Americans you usually get from cowboy films, isn't it? The reality is much more interesting. For a start, do you know why native Americans are called Indians? It happened by mistake. When Christopher Columbus landed in America in 1492, he had been trying to sail to India from Europe. Seeing land, he thought he had succeeded, and so called the people there Indians. Later they were called Red Indians, probably because some tribes painted their skins with red earth.

In prehistoric times, Indian hunters would stampede herds of buffalo towards the edge of a cliff until the terrified animals fell to their deaths. The Indians cut up the bodies for skins and meat, using stone knives.

Nineteenth-century Plains Indians

The first Americans, whom we call Indians, were nomadic hunters moving in from Asia in search of food.

North America:

West Coast

East Coast

The Great Plains

Atlantic Ocean

Mexico

Pacific Ocean

South America

8

A long, long trail

If you look at the little map opposite, you'll see that a very narrow strip of sea, the Bering Strait, separates the American continent from the north-east corner of Asia. Time and again, over thousands of years, the world has grown colder and then warmed up again.

1. Cheyenne in ceremonial headgear

During the cold periods, the Bering Strait froze over, so that it was possible to walk across. And that is what the nomadic hunters from Asia did, probably about ten thousand years ago. Some moved down into the mountains and jungles of South America, but many spread out into the plains and forests, mountains and deserts of the north, until there were over five hundred tribes, each with its own language and its own customs.

2. Iroquois

3. Pawnee

1. For many tribes the eagle was a holy bird.

2. The hunter ambushed the eagle when it came to the bait.

Pueblos and Navajos lived near the Mexican border in the south-west, a country of sunshine, deserts and canyons. The Pueblos watered the dry land and grew corn, tobacco and melons. Their villages were built into the cliff-sides, with some buildings several storeys high. You got to the top floors by ladder.

3. The hunter leapt up and caught the eagle.

4. Eagle-feathers in his war-bonnet lent the warrior the bird's courage.

The Pueblos' greatest enemies were the Navajos, who lived by hunting and fighting. When the Spanish asked who they were, the Pueblos replied 'Apaches' - enemies. Since prehistoric times, there had been no horses in North America. When the Spanish re-introduced them, the Navajos were the first of the tribes to master them. They were also fine craftsmen. They made pottery, jewellery and blankets.

The **Hurons** and the **Iroquois** lived in the north-east of the American continent, a land of woods, rivers and great lakes.

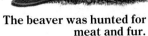

The beaver was hunted for meat and fur.

The Indians had all sorts of things to eat: fish and shellfish from the rivers and the sea, game from the forests, corn, beans and squash from the land. But they had to learn to weather the terrible winters: they wore thick furs to keep warm, and snow shoes so that they could still hunt, walking over even the deepest drifts. The birch trees around them were used for many different things: the long houses the Iroquois lived in, their light birch-bark canoes, their tools, their medicines.

Canadian Indians hunted moose.

They caught bear-cubs and trained them. Bears were among their favourite animals. Whether brown bears or grizzlies, they admired and respected them.

13

Seagoing Indians

All along the Pacific coast, Indian tribes lived off the riches of the sea: fish, shellfish, walrus, sea-lion, shark. The **Nootkas** and the **Makahs** even hunted whales from their heavy canoes, made of wood from the cedar trees which grow along the coast.

What is a totem pole?

It is a very tall wooden pole, carved with the faces of dead members of the tribe, of supernatural beings who had appeared to their ancestors, and of animals, such as bears or whales, which were sacred to the clan. All the great ceremonies of the West Coast Indians took place around a totem pole. Sometimes a totem pole was placed outside a house to protect the people living inside. An archway was carved at the base of the pole so that people could go in and out of the house.

The world of the Plains Indians:
Cheyennes, Arapahos, Kiowas, Sioux, Comanches, Blackfeet...

These are some of the tribes from the great plains of the central United States. Nomads, moving from place to place, and hunters, most of these people lived by following the great herds of buffalo as they moved across the plains. They hunted buffalo and depended on them for almost everything.

To build a tepee, the Indians arranged long poles in a big circle, tied together at the top. Then they covered them with buffalo skins, sewn together. Not all Plains Indians lived in tepees. Each tribe had its own kind of house: tents, mud huts or huts of dried grass.

An opening in the middle of the tepee let out the smoke from the fire. If it got too hot, the skins could be adjusted to let more air in.

How did the Indians manage without horses?

Up until the eighteenth century, they used dogs to help them carry their loads.

The travois, the oldest form of transport

From the moment the Spanish brought them, horses fascinated the Indians. They were like 'sacred dogs', according to the Comanches.

Drawings and sculptures honoured the memory of horses which had been killed in battle.

The Indians came to use horses all the time, for hunting, fighting and carrying things. The Indians caught them, bartered for them and even stole them. The more horses they owned, the richer they were. The Indians became very good riders. In a few days, they could catch a wild horse and train it to be ridden.

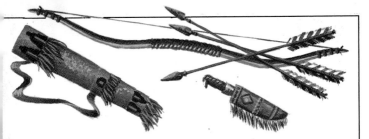

The American plains were once roamed by huge herds of **buffalo,** the American bison, animals a bit like enormous, hairy, wild cows. Before going hunting, the Indians would dance the buffalo-dance, to pacify the spirit of the buffalo. Then, on horseback, armed with bows and arrows, rifles and spears, they rode right into the herd and shot at point-blank range.

Hunters on foot sometimes covered themselves with wolf-skins in order to creep up on the herd.

Every part of a buffalo could be used: meat, fat, fur, skin, horns, bones and sinews.

Bead-embroidered moccasins

Meat was eaten fresh or dried.

Tanning leather

Turquoise
jewellery

Weaving
a blanket

Tanning skins, drying meat, building
tepees, weaving blankets: the wives,
or squaws, of these hunters, were
skilful craftswomen.

In the village the women were in charge of daily life. They looked after the food and the clothes, putting up and taking down tepees. A hunter might have several wives, and so a lot of children. Each birth was a cause of great joy for the whole tribe.

Learning skills

The young girls stayed in the village, where they played and learned to help their mothers. The young boys learned to hunt and shoot with a bow and arrow, and waited eagerly for the day when their fathers gave them their first ponies and took them out hunting.

The body had to be purified by going from hot to cold: from the sweat lodge to the river.

In order to be a hunter or a warrior, it was not enough to know how to ride or how to shoot a bow and arrow. Warriors had to be **initiated**. Everything, for the Indians, was linked to their religion. Stones, plants, animals and people were all the children of the one great spirit, which the Algonquins called the Great Manitou. This meant that everything that existed was worthy of equal respect. If a tree had to be cut down or an animal had to be killed, the spirits had first to be asked forgiveness. All these rules had be learned before a boy could become a warrior.

Smoking the pipe of peace was an important ritual. The Indians smoked tobacco to get nearer to the spirits.

The **shaman** occupied a very important position in the tribe. He was magician and doctor. According to Indian beliefs, he moved between the invisible world of the spirits and the world of people. A young boy would learn from him the mysteries of nature and the rules which had to be kept. Then, under the shaman's guidance, the boy was put through various trials: after his body had been purified, he had to spend several days alone without any food waiting for the spirits to visit him. A vision of an eagle, for instance, meant that the eagle would be his protective spirit. If he endured the trials bravely, he was accepted as a warrior.

There were all sorts
of games that they played with a ball.

The games Indians played. Even though their lives were not easy and they were often hungry, they still found time to laugh and play games. One of the most exciting was <u>lacrosse.</u>

A game of bones: you had to get the needle through the holes in the little bones.

Over a hundred men and boys might take part in the game! They were divided into two teams, each of which tried to hit the ball through the enemy goal with their racquets. One game could last an entire day.

Another game: two players tried to catch a rolling ring with their spears.

29

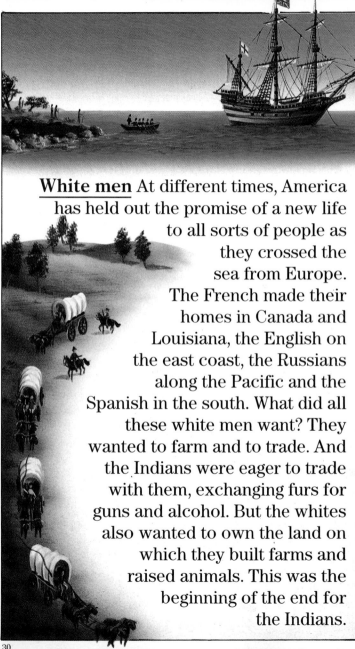

White men At different times, America has held out the promise of a new life to all sorts of people as they crossed the sea from Europe. The French made their homes in Canada and Louisiana, the English on the east coast, the Russians along the Pacific and the Spanish in the south. What did all these white men want? They wanted to farm and to trade. And the Indians were eager to trade with them, exchanging furs for guns and alcohol. But the whites also wanted to own the land on which they built farms and raised animals. This was the beginning of the end for the Indians.

In the middle of the nineteenth century
things began to happen faster and faster.
There were more and more white men.
They needed more and more land. The
Indians believed in the white men's
promises and treaties. All the same, they
tried to fight for their land and their food,
for the whites were wiping out the huge
buffalo herds the Indians needed to live on.

The Battle of Little Big Horn

On 25 June 1876, Sioux, Cheyennes, and Arapahos, under the leadership of Chief Sitting Bull and Chief Crazy Horse, fought the Americans and defeated General Custer. But this victory came too late. The Indians were worn out, starving, and disunited.

On 29 December 1890, the **Battle of Wounded Knee** marked the end of Indian resistance. 300 warriors were slaughtered in front of their women and children. The few who survived the massacre crept off to the bleak reservations. Many Indian tribes still live on reservations today.

To say: Comanche.
Imitate the movement
of a snake.

Cheyenne. Look
as if you are
cutting your finger.

Indian. Rub
your left hand
twice.

Pawnee. Palm
outwards, make a V
with your first two
fingers.

Crow. Put
your fist on
your forehead.

Sioux.
Pretend to cut
your throat.

Sign language

The tribes of the plains all spoke different
languages. In order to understand each
other, they invented a sign language, which
even the whites learned in the end.

You could use sign language not only to identify different
tribes, but to indicate different animals and objects.

1. Hello   2. How much?   3. Beaver   4. Friend
Often, the body was used as well as movements of the hand.
In order to say 'How much?' you have to stand sideways on.

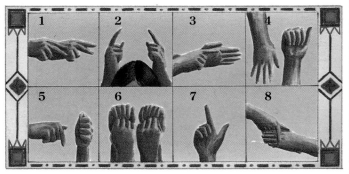

1. Dog   2. Buffalo   3. Cannot   4. Bad
5. Bow   6. Council   7. Moon   8. Horse

Hands, movements, face-painting, all meant different things.

Has already killed an enemy

War paint

Asking the spirits to send rain...

...or a thunderstorm.

Arm positions had meanings:
1. Has touched an enemy.
2. Has killed with his hands.
3. Has found the enemy.
4. Has killed with a rifle.
5. Has been wounded often.

Index

Pocket Worlds — building up into a child's first encyclopaedia: